# PUMPKIN PIE SPICE
## COOKBOOK

# PUMPKIN PIE SPICE
## COOKBOOK

### DELICIOUS RECIPES FOR SWEETS, TREATS, AND OTHER AUTUMNAL DELIGHTS

**STEPHANIE PEDERSEN**

*Photography by* **GUY AMBROSINO**

STERLING
New York

An Imprint of Sterling Publishing
387 Park Avenue South
New York, NY 10016

STERLING and the distinctive Sterling logo are registered trademarks of Sterling Publishing Co., Inc.

© 2014 by Stephanie Pedersen

Interior design by Allison Meierding

ISBN 978-1-4549-1398-6

Distributed in Canada by Sterling Publishing
c/o Canadian Manda Group, 165 Dufferin Street
Toronto, Ontario, Canada M6K 3H6
Distributed in the United Kingdom by GMC Distribution Services
Castle Place, 166 High Street, Lewes, East Sussex, England BN7 1XU
Distributed in Australia by Capricorn Link (Australia) Pty. Ltd.
P.O. Box 704, Windsor, NSW 2756, Australia

For information about custom editions, special sales, and premium and corporate purchases, please
contact Sterling Special Sales at 800-805-5489 or specialsales@sterlingpublishing.com.

Manufactured in China

2  4  6  8  10  9  7  5  3  1

www.sterlingpublishing.com

PRODUCED BY AUTHORSCAPE INC.

*To Leif Christian Pedersen,*
*Anders Gyldenvalde Pedersen, and*
*Axel Sune Lund Pedersen.*
*You are sweet. You are spicy. And I adore you!*

# CONTENTS

## IV. BREAKFAST

## V. SOUP, STEW, AND CHILI

## VI. MAIN DISHES

## VII. VEGGIE SIDES

## VIII. CONDIMENTS

## IX. PUMPKIN PIE SPICE BLENDS

# INTRODUCTION

**C**innamon, ginger, allspice, cloves, nutmeg **and mace:** Known collectively as Pumpkin Pie Spice Blend (or just Pumpkin Pie Spice) these warming spices sweeten our holiday baking while lending an intriguing flavor to savory cooking. Further, research has found that each of these spices—known as warming spices—has powerful healing benefits, including helping to lower blood pressure and cholesterol levels, serving to regulate blood sugar, and proving to boost immune system function.

While wonderful on their own, it's when you bring these spices together that true magic happens. Combined, these ingredients create a symphony of flavor and aroma so powerful, so deeply comforting, that the world smells like a special occasion.

# { COCKTAILS
## AND
# BEVERAGES }

# SPICYTINI

**MAKES 6 SERVINGS**

*This creative recipe makes a sweet cocktail. It's different. It's easy. And it's delicious.*

1   cup raw sugar
1   teaspoon pumpkin pie spice
1   cup water
    Juice of one lemon

    Splash vanilla extract
1½ cups vanilla vodka
1   liter seltzer, chilled

**1.** Make a simple sugar syrup by putting a small pot over medium heat, then mixing together the sugar and pumpkin pie spice with 1 cup water and the lemon juice.

**2.** Bring it to a boil, remove from the heat, and allow to cool for 1 hour. The syrup can be stored in the refrigerator for up to 2 weeks.

**3.** To a pitcher, add the vanilla extract, vanilla vodka and half the simple syrup. Stir until blended. Stir in the seltzer.

**4.** Pour drink into chilled martini glasses. Add more sugar syrup, to taste, if necessary.

# PUMPKIN SPICE CHAI LATTE

**MAKES 2 SERVINGS**

*This takes a bit more work than running out to your favorite upscale coffee joint, but it is so delicious that it's worth it!*

1½ cups milk (dairy, rice, coconut or any other type)

1½ cups water

1 teaspoon pumpkin pie spice blend of your choice

2 bags black tea

1 tablespoon pumpkin puree
  Optional: sweetener (choice; sugar, agave, maple syrup, honey, etc.)

**1.** In a saucepan on medium-low heat, gently simmer milk, water, and pumpkin pie spice.

**2.** Then turn off heat and steep tea bags for 2–3 minutes (or longer depending how strong you want the tea flavor).

**3.** When tea is desired strength, remove tea bags (squeezing out their liquid into the pot) and stir in pumpkin puree and optional sweetener. Pour into a cup or mug and enjoy.

# PUMPKIN SPICE COFFEE DRINK

## MAKES 2 SERVINGS

*If you are spending big bucks on frou-frou java joint drinks, save your cash and make your own. It's easy—plus, no weird ingredients. You control exactly what goes into this.*

½ cup milk (or use coconut milk or another non-dairy milk)

1 tablespoon unsweetened pumpkin puree

1 teaspoon granulated raw sugar, honey, or agave syrup

¼–½ teaspoon pumpkin pie spice

1 teaspoon vanilla extract

1½ cups hot brewed, strong coffee
Optional: 1 teaspoon granulated raw sugar, honey, or agave syrup, or more to taste

1. In a small pot, whisk together milk, pumpkin, sugar, spice, and vanilla.
2. Heat mixture over medium heat for about 2 minutes or until the mixture is hot and slightly frothy.
3. Pour the milk mixture into two tall mugs or large cups. Stir in hot coffee and optional sweetener. Stir.

### SPICE-KISSED COCOA

*Whether you like your hot chocolate made with a block of unsweetened chocolate and whole milk or prefer to stir an envelope of cocoa mix into a mug of scalding water, this tip is for you: Turn any cup of hot chocolate into something special by adding in ¼–½ teaspoon of your favorite pumpkin pie spice blend. I particularly like the basic blend and the Mexican blend for this.*

# VEGAN PUMPKIN SPICE NOG

## MAKES 4 SERVINGS

*This rich, creamy drink is so much healthier than traditional eggnog, and it's so delicious you just may end up drinking all four servings yourself. Feel free to increase the spices if you'd like. Use ¾ cup of cashews if you like your nog on the thin side. Use 1 cup if you like things thicker."*

¾–1 cup raw cashews

3 cups boiling water

2 cups cool water

1 15 ounce can of regular coconut milk (don't use "lite")

6 medjool dates, pitted

Splash vanilla extract

3 tablespoons (or more) dark or spiced rum

Dash salt

1½ teaspoons pumpkin pie spice

1. Place the cashews in medium bowl. Cover completely with boiling water and allow to soak for at least 30 minutes.

2. Drain and rinse cashews, then place the cashews with 2 cups cool water in a high-speed blender, such as VitaMix. Blend on high for 3 or so minutes or until very well blended and smooth.

3. Add remaining ingredients to the blender and blend on high again for another 3 minutes or until the dates are completely blended.

4. Serve immediately or place in the refrigerator. Will keep up to 2 days.

# SPICY PIE SMOOTHIE

**MAKES 4 SERVINGS**

*This is a fun, creamy treat that is also nutritious! You can make it even more healthful by tossing in a handful of walnuts, two tablespoons of chia seeds, ¼ of an avocado, or even a tablespoon or two of your favorite nut butter. Play with this!*

2   cups ice cubes
1½ cups vanilla coconut or almond
    or hazelnut milk
1   teaspoon pumpkin pie spice
    blend of your choice

½   teaspoon pure vanilla extract
3-5 pitted dates
½   cup pumpkin puree

1.  Place all ingredients into a high powered blender. Blend until well combined. Pour into your favorite glasses and enjoy cold.

---

### SPICY CIDER

*Want a fun, delicious, warm drink for your next party? Empty a liter, half-gallon, or gallon bottle of apple juice or apple cider into a stockpot set over a low flame, or into a crockpot set on a medium setting. Whisk in 1 or more teaspoons of a basic pumpkin pie spice blend, an optional squirt of lemon, and float in a few cinnamon sticks, whole cloves, and/or star anise pieces. Avoid boiling the mixture. Instead, keep the cider warm for as long as needed.*

# { APPETIZERS }

# SWEET SPICY FRUIT DIP

**MAKES 3 CUPS**

*This is a fun dip for fruit, crackers, or plain cookies. Kids love it! (You can even sandwich it between graham crackers or use it to frost cupcakes.)*

1  8-ounce package cream cheese, room temperature

2  cups confectioners' sugar, sifted

1  15-ounce can pure pumpkin puree (can use half applesauce or pearsauce if you'd like)

1  teaspoon pure vanilla extract

1  tablespoon pumpkin pie spice

**1.** In the bowl of a stand mixer, fitted with the paddle attachment, or in a large bowl with an electric mixer, beat cream cheese on medium-high speed until smooth and creamy; about 3 minutes.

**2.** Turn the mixer to low speed and gradually add confectioners' sugar. Increase speed to medium and continue mixing for another 2 minutes.

**3.** Reduce mixer speed and add in canned pumpkin, vanilla, and pumpkin pie spice. Mix until thoroughly combined.

**4.** Cover and chill for at least 3 hours.

# SAVORY PUMPKIN DIP

**MAKES 1¼ CUPS**

*Easy, tasty and healthful, this party dip comes together quickly with ingredients from the supermarket. It's great with whole grain crackers and veggie sticks.*

- 1  8-ounce tub hummus
- ¼  cup pumpkin puree
- ¼  teaspoon pumpkin pie spice

1. Stir together all ingredients until well-blended.

> **AMERICA'S OWN**
>
> *Only one spice found in pumpkin pie spice blends is native to the Americas: Allspice. Called "all" spice because its flavor has hints of cloves, cinnamon, ginger, mace, and nutmeg, allspice is an evergreen of the myrtle family. Today, allspice is grown in Jamaica, Mexico, Guatemala, Brazil, and the Leeward Islands.*

# PUMPKIN CROSTINI

## MAKES ABOUT 2 DOZEN APPETIZERS

*This recipe is a crowd pleaser and is easy enough that even any preteen children nearby can put it together.*

2  tablespoons extra virgin olive oil
1  clove garlic, roasted and minced
1  cup pumpkin purée.
1  teaspoon brown sugar
½  teaspoon pumpkin pie spice
   Salt and black pepper to taste

Optional garnishes: pine nuts, chopped pecans, chopped bacon, parmesan cheese
1  baguette, about 24 inches in length
   Couple tablespoons extra virgin olive oil

**1.** In a food processor fitted with the chopping blade, pulse together all ingredients except the garnishes, baguette and second addition of olive oil. Pulse until all ingredients are combined. Don't over-process—you do want a bit of texture.

**2.** Adjust the salt and pepper if necessary.

**3.** Make the crostini: Slice a baguette in ¾ inch slices and spread out flat on a rimmed baking sheet. Lightly coat the top of each bread surface with a small amount of olive oil. I used a pastry brush.

**4.** Broil in a broiler for about 30 seconds or until the tops start to turn light brown around the edges. Stay close and watch carefully—you don't want the toasts to burn!

**5.** Place a dollop of spread on each bread slice. Dress with optional garnishes, if desired.

# SWEET POTATO FRITTERS

## MAKES 6 SERVINGS

*Yum, fritters! These sweet, savory goodies take a bit of work, but are scrumptious!*

1-pound red-skinned sweet potato, baked in microwave or 350 oven until soft with skin on, or one cup of plain sweet potato puree

2 tablespoons (¼ stick) butter, melted

⅓ cup sugar

¾ teaspoon salt

½ teaspoon pumpkin pie spice

1 large egg

1 cup all purpose flour or gluten free all purpose flour

½ cup fresh bread crumbs made from crustless French bread or gluten free bread

1 tablespoon baking powder

Rice bran oil, coconut oil, or another high temperature vegetable oil for frying

1. Preheat oven to 350°F.

2. Spoon enough cooked sweet potato from skin into 1-cup measure to fill. Transfer 1 cup potato to medium bowl; add butter and mash well. Mix in sugar, salt, and pumpkin pie spice, then egg.

3. Whisk flour, breadcrumbs, and baking powder into potato mixture to make dough.

4. Pour enough oil into heavy medium saucepan to reach depth of 1 inch; heat oil to 325°F. Working in batches, drop dough by heaping teaspoonfuls into oil.

5. Fry until golden brown and cooked through, about 1½ minutes per side.

6. Using slotted spoon, transfer fritters to baking sheet; place in oven to keep warm. Repeat with remaining batter.

# SPICED NUTS

*Spiced nuts are a party favorite! Bet you can't eat just three!*

2 tablespoons unsalted butter
1 tablespoon sugar
½ teaspoon pumpkin pie spice

Dash salt
1 cup pecans or walnuts, or a combination of the two

1. In a small saucepan melt the butter over moderate heat.
2. Add the sugar, pumpkin pie spice, and salt, and stir until the sugar's dissolved. Add the nuts, stirring until golden, 2–4 minutes.
3. Transfer the nuts to a bowl to cool.

# GINGERBREAD CUPCAKES

## MAKES 12 CUPCAKES

*Soft, spicy gingerbread made as gorgeous cupcakes. These are irresistible!*

**CUPCAKES**
- ½ cup unsalted butter, softened to room temperature
- ½ cup dark brown sugar
- 1 large egg, at room temperature
- ½ cup milk, at room temperature*
- ½ cup molasses
- 1 teaspoon vanilla extract
- 1⅓ cups all-purpose flour
- ½ teaspoon baking powder
- ½ teaspoon baking soda
- ¼ teaspoon salt
- 2 teaspoons pumpkin pie spice

**OPTIONAL CREAM CHEESE FROSTING**
- 8 oz cream cheese, softened to room temperature
- ¼ cup unsalted butter, softened to room temperature
- 3 cups confectioners' sugar
- 1–2 tablespoons lemon juice or milk
- 1 teaspoon vanilla extract

1. Preheat oven to 350° F. Line 12-count muffin pan with cupcake liners. Set aside.

2. Make the cupcakes: In a large bowl using a handheld or stand mixer fitted with a paddle attachment, beat the butter and brown sugar together on medium speed until creamy.

3. Beat in the egg until combined, scraping down the sides and bottom of the bowl as needed. Beat in the milk, molasses, and vanilla on medium speed. Mixture will not look fully combined, and that's just fine.

Continues on next page >

**4.** In a medium bowl, toss the flour, baking powder, baking soda, salt, and pumpkin pie spice together until combined. With the mixer running on low speed, slowly pour the dry ingredients into the wet ingredients. Mix until just combined. Scrape down the sides and bottom of the bowl as needed.

**5.** Fill cupcake liners ⅔ of the way full, no more. Bake for 19–21 minutes or until a toothpick inserted in the center comes out mostly clean. Allow to cool completely before frosting.

**6.** Make the frosting: In a medium bowl using a handheld or stand mixer fitted with a paddle attachment, beat the cream cheese and butter together on medium speed until smooth, about 2 minutes.

**7.** Add the confectioners' sugar and 1 tablespoon of lemon juice. Beat for 2 minutes.

**8.** Add the vanilla and 1 more tablespoon more of lemon juice if necessary. Beat for 1 minute.

**9.** Frost cooled cupcakes immediately before serving.

### PUMPKIN PIE SPICE: THE ULTIMATE BAKING AID

*Whether you're making banana bread or ginger cookies, mincemeat pie or coffee cake, one or two teaspoons of your favorite pumpkin pie spice blend easily (and deliciously) replaces a recipe's recommended spices.*

# GELATIN SHOT TARTLETS

**MAKES 8 TARTLETS**

*You're right—Jell-O Shots ARE so '90s….but they're fun. And easy. This is a strictly adults-only treat.*

8  mini graham-cracker pie crusts
1  cup cold water
1  envelope (1 ounce) Knox
   unflavored gelatin
⅓  cup pumpkin puree
¼  cup granulated sugar

½  teaspoon pumpkin pie spice
½  cup vodka
¼  cup cold water
½  tablespoon cold heavy cream
   Optional: fresh whipped cream,
   for serving

**1.** Arrange the piecrusts on a baking sheet. Place 1 cup cold water in the top of a double boiler and sprinkle the gelatin over the top. Let stand for three minutes.

**2.** Keeping the gelatin mixture in the double boiler, heat the gelatin mixture to a gentle simmer until the granules have dissolved.

**3.** Add the pumpkin, sugar, and pumpkin pie spice and heat, stirring occasionally, until the pumpkin and sugar are completely melted.

**4.** Remove from heat and cool for 30 minutes.

**5.** In a medium bowl, combine the vodka with ¼ cup cold water and the heavy cream. Whisk in the pumpkin mixture and immediately divide it among the piecrusts. Chill until firm, at least 4 hours.

**6.** To serve, slice the pies into quarters and top with optional whipped cream before serving.

# HEALTHY PUMPKIN PUDDING

**MAKES 6 SERVINGS**

*Easier to make than pumpkin pie, this simple pudding is healthy enough to enjoy for breakfast.*

2  cups 2% reduced-fat milk
¾  cup dark brown sugar
¼  cup cornstarch
2  large eggs

1  cup pumpkin puree
¼  teaspoon salt
¼  teaspoon pumpkin-pie spice

**1.** In a large saucepan, whisk milk, sugar, and cornstarch; bring to a boil. Boil 3 minutes, whisking constantly.

**2.** In a large bowl, beat eggs with a whisk. Gradually add half the hot milk mixture to the beaten eggs.

**3.** Add milk-egg mixture to pan and cook over medium heat 3 minutes, or until thick, whisking constantly.

**4.** Remove from heat; stir in pumpkin, salt, and pumpkin-pie spice.

**5.** Spoon evenly into 6 custard cups.

**6.** Let cool, and chill for about 30 minutes, or until pudding is set.

# SPICY APPLE CHEESECAKE

## MAKES 10 SERVINGS

*Pumpkin pie spice and delicious apples give cheesecake a fresh, autumnal flavor. This is a must-try for anyone who has a hard time deciding between apple pie and cheesecake at dessert time.*

- 1 cup graham cracker crumbs
- ½ cup finely chopped walnuts
- 3 tablespoons white sugar
- ½ teaspoon ground pumpkin pie spice
- ¼ cup unsalted butter, melted
- 2 (8 ounce) packages cream cheese, softened
- ½ cup white sugar
- 2 large eggs
- ½ teaspoon vanilla extract
- ⅓ cup white sugar
- 1 teaspoon pumpkin pie spice
- 4 cups tart apples, peeled, cored, and thinly sliced
- ¼ cup chopped walnuts

1. Preheat oven to 350° F.

2. In a large bowl, stir together the graham cracker crumbs, ½ cup finely chopped walnuts, 3 tablespoons sugar, ½ teaspoon pumpkin pie spice, and melted butter; press into the bottom of a 9 inch springform pan. Bake in preheated oven for 10 minutes.

3. In a large mixing bowl, combine cream cheese and ½ cup sugar. Mix at medium speed until smooth.

4. Beat in eggs, one at a time, mixing well after each addition.

5. Blend in vanilla.

Continues on next page >

**6.** Pour filling into the baked crust.

**7.** In a small bowl, stir together ⅓ cup sugar and ½ teaspoon pumpkin pie spice. Toss the spice-sugar with the apples to coat.

**8.** Spoon apple mixture over cream cheese layer and sprinkle with ¼ cup chopped walnuts.

**9.** Bake in preheated oven for 60 to 70 minutes.

**10.** With a knife, loosen cake from rim of pan. Let cool, then remove the rim of pan.

**11.** Chill cake before serving.

### HOW MANY CALORIES?

*If you were to eat one teaspoon of pumpkin pie spice, you'd be consuming 6 calories. You'd also get 1% of your body's daily requirement for calcium and Vitamin C, and 2% of your requirement for iron.*

# { BREAKFAST }

# SPICY WAFFLES

**MAKES ABOUT 8 WAFFLES**

*Pumpkin waffles are a staple in many upscale diners. This fluffy version can be made with sweet potato puree or thick unsweetened applesauce.*

1½ cups all-purpose flour
3 teaspoons baking powder
½ teaspoon baking soda
2 teaspoons pumpkin pie spice
1 pinch salt
2 large eggs
¼ cup firmly packed brown sugar
1 cup canned pumpkin puree (or sweet potato puree or thick, unsweetened applesauce)

1⅔ cups dairy or coconut milk
4 tablespoons butter or coconut oil, melted and cooled
Optional toppings: Sautéed apples, cranberry sauce, jam, honey, maple syrup, powdered sugar, applesauce, chopped nuts

1. Mix together flour, baking powder, baking soda, pumpkin pie spice, and salt in large bowl.
2. In a second bowl, add eggs, sugar, pumpkin, milk, and butter; beat well.
3. Gently fold in the flour mixture.
4. Cook according to your waffle iron directions.
5. Top with your choice of ingredients.

# SPICED FLAPJACKS

## MAKES 6 PANCAKES

*Who doesn't love pancakes? These gorgeous treats have a rich, spicy flavor and a warm golden color.*

1¼ cups all-purpose flour
2 tablespoons sugar
2 teaspoons baking powder
1½ teaspoons pumpkin pie spice
½ teaspoon salt
1 cup dairy or coconut milk
6 tablespoons canned pumpkin puree

2 tablespoons melted butter or coconut oil
1 large egg
Optional toppings: Sautéed apples, cranberry sauce, jam, honey, maple syrup, powdered sugar, applesauce, chopped nuts

1. Whisk flour, sugar, baking powder, pumpkin pie spice, and salt in a bowl.
2. In a separate bowl whisk together milk, pumpkin, melted butter, and egg.
3. Fold mixture into dry ingredients.
4. Spray or grease a skillet and heat over medium heat: pour in ¼ cup batter for each pancake.
5. Cook pancakes about 3 minutes per side. Serve with butter and syrup.

### SPICY BREAKFAST PORRIDGE
*Dress up any hot cereal—from oatmeal to cream of wheat to corn grits—with ¼ teaspoon or more of your favorite pumpkin pie spice blend.*

# WHEAT-FREE BREAKFAST COOKIE

## MAKES BETWEEN 8 AND 10 COOKIES

*Cookies for breakfast? Absolutely, as long as they're protein-packed, fiber-filled, and nutrient dense like these wheat-free beauties. You'll love the sweet, spicy flavor and the moist texture.*

- 2 cups quick oats (not whole or old fashioned oats)
- ¾ teaspoon salt
- 1 teaspoon pumpkin pie spice
- 1 cup almond butter, cashew butter, peanut butter, or sunflower seed butter
- ¼ cup Grade B maple syrup (Dark Amber)
- ¼ cup thick unsweetened applesauce, pumpkin puree, or sweet potato puree
- 1 large banana, mashed
- ½ cup dried fruit of choice, chopped
- ½ cup shelled sunflower or pumpkin seeds
- ½ cup finely chopped walnuts
- 1 tablespoon chia

1. Preheat oven to 325° F. Line a large cookie sheet with parchment paper or a silicone baking mat. Set aside.
2. Combine all of the ingredients into the large bowl of a stand mixer. Mix until all of the ingredients are combined. The dough will be quite stiff.
3. Take ¼ cup of dough and drop onto prepared cookie sheet. Slightly flatten the tops into desired thickness. The cookies will not spread in the oven.
4. Bake for 15–16 minutes or until edges are slightly brown. Allow to cool on the cookie sheets completely. Cookies stay fresh at room temperature for 1 week and can be frozen.

# MY FAVORITE GRANOLA

**MAKES 10 CUPS**

*Granola is easy to make and fun to personalize. This version is scented with pumpkin pie spice and contains all kinds of healthy ingredients like hemp and chia. Enjoy for breakfast, for snacks, or for topping yogurt, puddings, and other foods.*

7½ cups rolled oats

1 cup walnuts, chopped

1 cup golden raisin

¼ cup ground flax seed

¼ cup ground hemp seed

2 tablespoon chia seed

½ cup brown sugar

½ cup coconut oil

½ cup honey

½ tablespoon pumpkin pie spice

1 tablespoon vanilla

1. Preheat oven to 275°F In big bowl, combine oats, raisins, nuts, flaxseed, hemp, and chia.

2. In microwavable bowl, or in a small pot, blend together brown sugar, oil, honey, and pumpkin pie spice.

3. Cook on high in microwave or heat pot over medium heat until mixture starts bubbling. Remove, add vanilla, and stir.

4. Pour over oat mixture and mix well.

5. Thinly spread on 2 or more baking sheets. Bake for 15 minutes.

6. Stir and return to oven for an additional 10 to 15 minutes or until oats are toasted.

7. Cool thoroughly.

8. Store in an airtight container in the fridge.

# MORNING SPICE MUFFINS

## MAKES 12 MUFFINS

*In the 1980s and 1990s, Morning Glory Muffins were all the rage. They're just as delicious today, and are made even easier by using pumpkin pie spice.*

1⅓ cups all-purpose flour

¾ cup sugar

1½ teaspoons baking soda

⅓ teaspoon salt

1½ teaspoons pumpkin pie spice

⅔ cup coconut oil

2 large eggs

1¼ teaspoons vanilla extract

1⅓ cups grated peeled apples (about 1 large apple)

⅓ cup shredded carrot

⅓ cup raisins or chopped dried fruit

⅓ cup flaked coconut

Optional: ⅓ cup chopped walnuts or pecans (optional)

1. Preheat oven to 350° F.
2. Line 12 muffin cups with paper muffin liners.
3. In a large bowl whisk together flour, sugar, baking soda, salt, and pumpkin pie spice.
4. In a separate bowl, mix oil, eggs, and vanilla.
5. Blend wet ingredients into dry and gently stir until ingredients are combined.
6. Fold in the apples, carrots, raisins, coconut, and nuts.
7. Fill muffin cups ⅔ full.
8. Bake 25–30 minutes or until a toothpick inserted in center comes out clean.

## THE FIRST MENTION OF PUMPKIN PIE SPICE

*The basics of pumpkin pie go back to writings in Medieval times sometime before the 1500's, where pumpkin was stewed with sugar and fragrant spices and wrapped in pastry.*

# { SOUP, STEW, and CHILI }

# SPICY PUMPKIN-COCONUT BISQUE

## MAKES 4 SERVINGS

*Light, deeply nutritious, delicious, and just exotic enough to be exciting, this pumpkin soup is fantastic. And easy! It freezes well, too—if you happen to have any leftovers.*

1  tablespoon butter
1  large onion, chopped
1  or 2 large garlic cloves, minced
2  cups strong chicken or vegetable broth
2  (14 ounce) cans pumpkin puree
1  (14 ounce) can regular coconut milk

2  tablespoons orange or lemon juice
2  teaspoons ground ginger
2  teaspoons pumpkin pie spice
2  teaspoons chili powder
   Optional garnish: chopped chives, parsley, cilantro or pumpkin seeds

1. Melt the butter in a large pot over medium heat. Add the onion and garlic. Stir until softened, about 5 minutes.

2. Add the broth to the onions and garlic. Cook 2 to 3 minutes.

3. Stir the pumpkin puree, coconut milk, orange juice, ginger, pumpkin pie spice, and chili powder into the liquid. Bring the soup to a simmer, and cook until heated through, 5 to 7 minutes.

4. Working in batches, pour soup into a blender until the blender's pitcher is no more than half full. Puree soup until completely smooth, returning pureed soup to pot. Continue until all soup is blended. Alternately, use a stick blender to puree the soup in the pot.

5. Warm the pureed soup over medium heat. Bring to a simmer and cook another 10 minutes.

# AUTUMN CHILI

## MAKES 8 SERVINGS

*This hearty chili is yummy, healthy, and versatile. It also freezes well, for those of you who love cooking ahead. Play around with the spices to see what you like.*

- 2 lbs ground beef (you can also use ground turkey, pork, or a combination of your choosing)
- 1 large onion, chopped
- 2 large garlic cloves, minced
- 1 red bell pepper, chopped
- 30 ounce can (or 3.5 cups cooked) kidney, pinto, or black beans, drained
- 3 28-ounce cans diced tomatoes with juice
- ½ cup pumpkin puree, either homemade or canned
- 1½ tablespoon pumpkin pie spice (this is especially good with the Mexican Pumpkin Pie Spice Blend on page 92)
- 1½ tablespoon chili powder
- Salt and pepper to taste
- Optional: 2 tablespoons minced cilantro for garnish

1. In a large pot over medium heat, cook beef until brown.
2. Stir in garlic, onion, and red pepper and cook 5 minutes.
3. Stir in beans, diced tomatoes and pumpkin puree.
4. Season with pumpkin pie spice, chili powder, salt and pepper.
5. Simmer for 1 hour.
6. Sprinkle with chopped cilantro, if desired.

# SWEET & SOUR LENTIL SOUP

## MAKES 8 SERVINGS

*This is a basic lentil soup recipe that creates an outstanding soup! Try it!*

1 tablespoon extra virgin olive oil
1 large onion, chopped
3 large cloves garlic, minced
1 carrot, diced
1 celery stalk, diced
2 medium sweet potatoes, peeled and cut into ½ inch cubes
1½ cups dried brown lentils
10 cups chicken or vegetable broth (about five 15-ounce cans)

2 (15 ounce) cans diced tomatoes with juice
2 bay leaves
1 teaspoon dried thyme
1 tablespoon Pumpkin Pie Spice (I especially like the Jamaican Pumpkin Pie Spice here)
Salt and pepper, to taste
2 cups chopped fresh spinach
½ tablespoon (or more, if desired) apple cider vinegar

**1.** In a large pot, heat the olive oil. Add the onion and garlic. Sauté until onion is tender and garlic is light brown in color.

**2.** Add carrot, celery, and sweet potatoes. Cook until vegetables soften, about 5–7 minutes.

**3.** Stir in the lentils and broth. Add the diced tomatoes, bay leaves, thyme, and pumpkin pie spice. Season with salt and pepper and stir. Cook on medium-low heat for about 35–40 minutes or until lentils are cooked.

**4.** Add the fresh spinach and vinegar and stir. Remove bay leaves and add salt and pepper if necessary.

# BEEF-PUMPKIN STEW

## MAKES 6 SERVINGS

*This is a classic beef stew given a twist with pumpkin and pumpkin pie spice.*
*This is an ideal autumn or winter dish, served alone or ladled over quinoa,*
*couscous, polenta, or mashed potatoes.*

3  lbs stew beef trimmed into
   1¼-inch chunks
   Salt and fresh ground black pepper
1  tablespoon olive oil
1  large onion, finely chopped
2  sprigs fresh thyme
3  bay leaves
6  cloves garlic, finely chopped
⅓  cup dry red wine (such as merlot)
2  tablespoons red wine vinegar

2  large carrots, peeled and cut
   into chunks
1  (15 ounce) can diced tomatoes
⅓  cup beef or chicken stock
1  lb pumpkin or butternut squash,
   peeled, seeded, and cut into
   ¾-inch chunks
2  teaspoons pumpkin pie spice
   (I like the homemade Basic
   Pumpkin Pie Spice Blend recipe,
   on page 86, for this)

1. Season the beef generously with salt and pepper.

2. In a large, heavy frying pan over medium-high heat, warm the olive oil,
add the beef, and braise it until browned on all sides (about 8 min total).

3. Using a slotted spoon, remove the beef to a plate.

4. Pour off most of the fat from the pan, return to the medium-high heat and sauté
the onion, thyme, and bay leaves until the onion begins to brown (about 6 min).

Continues on next page >

**5.** Add garlic, cook 1 additional minute.

**6.** Pour in the wine and vinegar and stir to dislodge any flavorful browned bits on the bottom of the pan.

**7.** Transfer the contents to a slow cooker with the meat, carrots, tomatoes, and stock.

**8.** Cover and cook on low setting for approx 5 hours.

**9.** Add the pumpkin or squash chunks and pumpkin pie spice over the top of the beef, recover and continue to cook the stew for 3 more hours. The beef and pumpkin should be very tender.

**10.** Remove and discard thyme sprigs, and bay leaves, skim off the fat.

### INSTANT GOURMET SOUP

*Canned and boxed soups can go upscale with a little help from our favorite spice blend. When heating up a pumpkin or winter squash-flavored soup, simply stir in ½ teaspoon or more of your favorite pumpkin pie spice blend. Yum!*

# CARROT SPICE BISQUE

## MAKES 5 SERVINGS

*I began pureeing root veggies and nut butters into soups when my oldest son was an infant. This carrot-almond butter version was his favorite. I love it, too. (I love it even more because it's incredibly economical and outrageously easy.)*

2   tablespoons butter, coconut oil, almond oil or extra virgin olive oil
3   cups chopped carrots
½   cup chopped onion
½   cup chopped celery
2   teaspoons minced fresh ginger
1   or 2 garlic cloves, minced
4   cups chicken or vegetable broth
½   teaspoon pumpkin pie spice
½   teaspoon salt (or to taste, depending upon how salty your broth is)
¼   cup almond butter (any type is fine)
1½  tablespoons natural soy sauce (shoyu or tamari)
    Black pepper, to taste

1. Warm butter or oil in a large soup pot over medium heat. Add carrots, onion, celery, ginger, and garlic. Sauté until vegetables are just softened and onions begin to get translucent.

2. Add broth and simmer, about 20 minutes, until carrots are tender.

3. Cool to room temperature.

4. In a blender (do this in batches if necessary), puree soup with pumpkin pie spice, salt, almond butter, soy sauce and black pepper. Continue blending until soup is silky smooth.

5. Garnish finished soup with chopped almonds and/or chopped parsley and a dusting of pumpkin pie spice, if desired.

# { MAIN DISHES }

# CARIBBEAN SLOWCOOKER PULLED PORK

## MAKES 6 SERVINGS

*If you love pulled pork, you need to try this exotic (and nutritious) version featuring the flavors of Jamaica. In my house we serve this over turned cornmeal (kind of a Jamaican-style polenta), grits or mashed potatoes, but it's also great tucked into a whole wheat roll and dressed with your favorite condiments and garnishes.*

2¼ lb boneless pork roast
(shoulder, butt or picnic roast)
1 onion, quartered
4 cloves garlic
1 cup pumpkin puree
¼ cup unfiltered apple cider vinegar
¼ cup dark spiced rum
2 tablespoons Worcestershire sauce
2 jalapenos
1½ inch piece fresh ginger, peeled

1 teaspoon Jamaican Pumpkin Pie
Spice Blend
1 teaspoon ground thyme
Salt and black pepper to taste
Optional for serving: Whole wheat
bun, mashed potatoes, turned cornmeal, grits, or your favorite grain
Optional garnish: Sliced red onions,
avocadoes and/or tomatoes,
pickles, etc.

1. Place pork in a large casserole or food storage container.
2. In a blender or food processor, puree all ingredients except the pork.
3. Pour over the pork in a marinating container or resealable bag.
Refrigerate overnight.
4. The next morning, pour everything into a slow cooker. Cook on low 8–10 hours.
5. When the pork is thoroughly cooked, shred it in the slow-cooker with two forks. Toss to evenly distribute the sauce. Serve on rolls or over polenta or mashed potatoes.

# PUMPKIN SLOPPY JOES

## MAKES 8 SERVINGS

*The "Manwhich" goes gourmet, thanks to pumpkin pie spice. Delicious!*

1 pound ground beef
½ cup chopped onion
2 garlic cloves, minced
1 cup canned pumpkin
1 can (8 ounces) tomato sauce
2 tablespoons brown sugar
2 tablespoons prepared mustard

2 teaspoons chili powder
½ teaspoon (or more, if desired) pumpkin pie spice
½ teaspoon salt
8 whole grain rolls or hamburger buns, split

1. In a large skillet, cook the beef, onion, and garlic over medium heat until meat is no longer pink; drain.
2. Stir in the pumpkin, tomato sauce, brown sugar, mustard, chili powder, and salt. Bring to a boil. Reduce heat; simmer, uncovered, for 10 minutes.
3. Spoon meat mixture onto buns.

> ### WOW, THAT'S A LOT OF CINNAMON!
> In 2005 the largest pumpkin pie ever was made and weighed over 2020 pounds. It used 900 pounds of cooked pumpkin, 300 pounds of sugar, 155 dozen eggs, 62 gallons of evaporated milk, 300 pounds of sugar, 3.5 pounds of salt, 7 pounds of cinnamon, and 2 pounds of pumpkin pie spice.

# BLACK BEAN MOLE BURGERS

**MAKES 2 BURGERS**

*Fun, fast and fabulous, this tasty burger is packed with nutrient dense superfoods.*

1 cup cooked or canned black beans, drained and rinsed

1 (or more) large garlic cloves, minced

⅓ cup canned pumpkin

1 tablespoon all-purpose flour, gluten free flour or whole wheat pastry flour

½ teaspoon cumin

½ teaspoon pumpkin pie spice

¼ teaspoon chili powder

1 tablespoon (or more) chopped cilantro

A bit of oil for the pan

1. Combine all ingredients in a bowl and mash them together, or pulse them two or three times in a food processor, being careful not to puree.

2. Once mashed/mixed to desired consistency, form into two patties. Cook in a lightly oiled skillet until golden brown on each side.

# AFGHANI-STYLE SWEET STEW

## MAKES 4 SERVINGS

*I am embarrassed to admit that I came late to Afghani food. I was in my early 30s and had wandered into a neighborhood Afghani restaurant. I could not believe the delicious vegetable blends—especially all the creative ways with winter squash. This stew, which is served over millet, couscous, brown rice, quinoa, or another grain, is filling, dense with phytonutrients for a strong immune system, vegetarian, and delicious.*

2½ cup chopped onion

1 tablespoon extra virgin olive oil

1½ tablespoons minced ginger root

3 large cloves garlic, minced

1½ teaspoon ground coriander

½ teaspoon ground cumin

1 teaspoon Scandinavian Pumpkin Pie Spice Blend (page 88)

½ teaspoon salt

Pinch of black pepper

1 teaspoon brown sugar

8 cups diced butternut squash, cut into 1½-inch dice

1½ cups diced tomatoes (fresh or canned, drained first)

⅓ cup dried black currants

Optional: ⅓ cup toasted almonds sliced or coarsely chopped

1. Add olive oil to a large saucepan over medium-high heat. Sauté onions for about 5 minutes, until softened.

2. Add ginger and garlic and sauté about 4 minutes.

3. Stir in coriander, cumin, Scandinavian Pumpkin Pie Spice Blend, salt, pepper and brown sugar, until well blended.

**4.** Add the squash, tomatoes and currents and allow to simmer for 30 minutes, or until the squash is quite soft.

**5.** Adjust salt and pepper—and other seasonings, if desired. Garnish with optional almonds, if desired.

**6.** Serve over a bed of millet, couscous, brown rice, quinoa, or another grain.

## WHAT IS CORIANDER?

*Coriander seed is the dried ripe fruit of the herb, Coriandum sativum, a member of the parsley family. Coriander spans the culinary globe lending it's bright, slightly citrusy flavor to a variety of cuisines, including Southwestern, Latin, Caribbean, Mexican, Mediterranean, North African, Indian, and Southeast Asian. (Coriandum sativum's green, fresh-tasting leaves—known as cilantro—are another popular flavoring agent). However, coriander's most famous role may be as the sugarplums mentioned in 'Twas The Night Before Christmas: Coated with sugar and colored pink and white, coriander comfit—or sugarplums—were a favorite holiday sweet.*

# { VEGGIE SIDES }

# PICKLED PUMPKIN

## MAKES 8 SERVINGS

*This is an old-fashioned way of enjoying (and preserving) pumpkin. It adds a light, refreshing touch to heavy meals.*

1  pound peeled and diced pumpkin
1 ¼ cups white sugar
1  teaspoon pumpkin pie spice

1 ¼ cups distilled white vinegar
1  cinnamon stick
3  or 4 whole cloves

**1.** Place the pumpkin in a large, deep bowl.

**2.** In a large saucepan, mix the sugar, pumpkin pie spice, vinegar, cinnamon sticks, and cloves. Boil 5 minutes. Pour the hot liquid over the pumpkin in the bowl. Cover and set aside 8 hours, or overnight.

**3.** Strain the liquid into a large saucepan. Boil 5 minutes. Remove the cinnamon sticks and cloves, leaving a few bits for decoration. Place the pumpkin back into the liquid and return to boiling. Boil 5 minutes, or until pumpkin is transparent but crisp. Allow the mixture to cool. Transfer to sterile jars and refrigerate.

# SPICE-RUBBED ROASTED VEGGIES

## MAKES 4 TO 6 SERVINGS

*Every home cook needs a great roasted veggie recipe. This is one of the best around.*

2 lb winter squash or pumpkin, parsnips, carrots, beets, or a mix of these

2 medium red or yellow onions, quartered

1 tablespoon extra-virgin olive oil

1 teaspoon pumpkin pie spice
Salt and black pepper to taste

1. Preheat the oven to 400° F.
2. Peel vegetables and cut them into 1-inch chunks.
3. Toss vegetables and onions in olive oil in a large bowl and season with pumpkin pie spice, salt and pepper.
4. Spread the pieces out in a single layer on one or two roasting pans/trays so that the vegetables don't touch.
5. Roast until the veggies are lightly browned and just tender, 45 minutes to 1 hour, depending on the vegetable.
6. Remove and toss with additional olive oil if desired and adjust salt and pepper.

> **DID YOU KNOW...**
> 54% of all pumpkin pie spice sales worldwide occur in November.

# SWEET POTATO MASH-UP

## MAKES 4 SERVINGS

*One day I was brainstorming on ways to use the last of some allspice berries I'd brought back from Jamaica. "Why not use it to dress up some mashed sweet potatoes?" I thought to myself. Voila! A new side dish was born!*

1 pounds sweet potatoes, peeled and cut into 2-inch pieces

2 tablespoons coconut oil

½ cup canned coconut milk

½ teaspoon salt

½ teaspoon Jamaican Pumpkin Pie Spice (page 89)

1. Place the sweet potatoes in a large pot. Add just enough cold water to cover them.

2. Place pot over high heat and bring to a boil. Cook sweet potatoes until tender, about 15 minutes. Turn burner off.

3. Drain and return to the potatoes to the pot on the stovetop. Immediately, while the sweet potatoes are still warm, add the remaining ingredients.

4. Using a potato masher, smash everything together until smoothish in texture and well-blended.

**Alternate recipe:** For a more traditional take on mashed sweet potatoes, use butter instead of coconut oil, regular dairy milk in place of the coconut milk and opt for a traditional pumpkin pie spice blend (such as the Basic Pumpkin Pie Spice Blend on page 86).

# HEALTHY WINTER GRATIN

**MAKES 6 SERVINGS**

*Everyone loves a gratin! This one goes together quickly, is highly nourishing, and is addictive.*

2 medium parsnips (about 4 medium)
½ medium celery root
½ pound sweet potatoes
¾ pound russet (baking) potatoes
1 teaspoons salt
1 teaspoon finely chopped garlic

½ teaspoon black pepper
¼ teaspoon pumpkin pie spice
¼ cup reduced-sodium chicken broth
¾ cups heavy cream
Optional garnish: Chopped parsley or chives

1. Put oven rack in upper third of oven and preheat oven to 400°F.
2. Peel vegetables and cut into one-inch cubes. Transfer to a large bowl.
3. Add salt, garlic, pepper, pumpkin pie spice, broth, and cream, tossing to combine.
4. Transfer to gratin dish or casserole dish, spreading evenly.
5. Cover gratin with a lid, a piece or parchment, or foil. Bake until gratin is bubbling all over and vegetables are tender when pierced with a knife, about 30 to 40 minutes.
6. Uncover grain and cook for 5 to 10 more minutes to create a golden brown surface.

{ CONDIMENTS }

# SWEET-SPICY HOLIDAY RELISH

## MAKES ABOUT 4 CUPS

*This is very different and absolutely delicious! Eat with your holiday turkey or lamb. It's also great on sandwiches.*

1½-pound butternut squash
1 cup orange juice
1 cup sugar
¼ teaspoon dried hot red pepper flakes

1 teaspoons pumpkin pie spice
3 navel oranges
1 tablespoon balsamic vinegar
1 scallion, minced

1. Halve squash lengthwise and discard seeds. Peel squash and cut into ½-inch dice.

2. In a saucepan bring juice and sugar to a boil with red pepper flakes, stirring to dissolve sugar. Add squash and pumpkin pie spice and simmer, covered, for 5 minutes or until squash is tender. Transfer mixture to a bowl and cool.

3. With a serrated knife cut peel and pith from oranges and working over bowl of squash mixture cut orange sections free from membranes, letting sections drop into squash mixture and squeezing excess juice from membranes into mixture. Stir vinegar into relish. Relish may be prepared up to this point 1 week ahead and chilled, covered.

4. With a slotted spoon, transfer relish to a serving bowl and stir in scallion. Serve relish chilled or at room temperature with poultry or lamb.

# SAVORY CRANBERRY CHUTNEY

## MAKES 2 CUPS

*Savory, sweet and stunning, this is addictive!*

5  shallots (6 oz), coarsely chopped
1½ tablespoons extra virgin olive oil
1  (12-oz) bag fresh or frozen
   cranberries
⅔  cup sugar
¼  cup apple cider vinegar

1  teaspoon minced garlic
1  teaspoon minced peeled
   fresh ginger
½  teaspoon (or more) pumpkin pie spice
½  teaspoon salt
½  teaspoon black pepper

1. Cook shallots in oil in a 3-quart heavy saucepan over moderate heat, stirring occasionally, until softened.
2. Stir in remaining ingredients. Simmer, stirring occasionally, until berries just pop, 10 to 12 minutes.
3. Cool to room temperature before serving.

> **DID YOU KNOW....**
> *The word "chutney" is derived from the Indian word "chatni," which is an Indian condiment made of ingredients that have been crushed together with a mortar and pestle.*

# SPICY KETCHUP

**MAKES 2¾ CUPS**

*When you find out how easy it is to make your own delicious, spicy ketchup, you'll never go back to the bottled condiment.*

- 1 (28-to 32-ounce) can whole tomatoes in juice
- 1 medium onion, chopped
- 4 garlic cloves, chopped
- 2 tablespoons vegetable oil
- 1 teaspoon chili powder
- ½ teaspoon paprika
- ½ teaspoon pumpkin pie spice
- 1 tablespoon tomato paste
- ½ cup packed light brown sugar
- ½ cup cider vinegar

1. Purée tomatoes with juice in a blender until smooth.
2. Cook onion and garlic in oil with ¼ teaspoon salt in a 4-quart heavy saucepan over medium heat, stirring occasionally, until golden, about 8 minutes.
3. Add spices and ½ teaspoon pepper and cook, stirring frequently, 1 minute.
4. Add tomato purée, tomato paste, brown sugar, and vinegar, and simmer, uncovered, stirring occasionally, until very thick, 45 to 55 minutes (stir more frequently toward end of cooking to prevent scorching).
5. Purée ketchup in blender until smooth (use caution when blending hot liquids). Chill at least 2 hours (for flavors to develop).
6. *Note:* Ketchup keeps, chilled, 1 month.

# { PUMPKIN PIE SPICE BLENDS }

*These can be used teaspoon for teaspoon, tablespoon for tablespoon anywhere you'd use a commercially prepared pumpkin pie spice blend. If you want to shake up your tastebuds feel free to exchange one of the more exotic pumpkin pie spice blends for the basic recipe.*

# BASIC PUMPKIN PIE SPICE BLEND

**MAKES 8 TABLESPOONS**

*This is your basic, yummy pumpkin pie spice. It's similar to most of the pre-made spice blends you can buy at the supermarket, in specialty stores and from bakery suppliers. Feel free to play with it, omitting any spice you may not like, or increasing any of those you adore. (Just go easy on the nutmeg, which can taste bitter in large quantities.)*

4 tablespoons ground cinnamon

2 tablespoons ground ginger

3 teaspoons ground allspice

2 teaspoons ground nutmeg

½ teaspoon ground cloves

½ teaspoon ground mace

1. In a small dry bowl, whisk ingredients together.
2. Place in an airtight container and store in a dry, cool, dark place.

---

**WHAT IS MACE?**

*Mace is the covering of the nutmeg seed. It tastes similar to nutmeg, with overtones of cinnamon and black pepper.*

---

# SCANDINAVIAN PUMPKIN PIE SPICE BLEND

**MAKES 8 TABLESPOONS**

*In Denmark and Sweden, cardamom is a baking staple. Its warm, toasty, aromatic and slightly mysterious flavor lends an exotic quality to this wonderful splice blend.*

4½ tablespoons ground cinnamon

2½ tablespoons ground ginger

2 teaspoons ground allspice

2 teaspoons ground cardamom

½ teaspoon ground fennel

½ teaspoon ground dried lemon zest

1. In a small dry bowl, whisk ingredients together.
2. Place in an airtight container and store in a dry, cool, dark place.

**WHAT IS CARDAMOM?**

*A member of the ginger family, cardamom is a seed pod that can be used whole or ground. Its pungent flavor and aroma boasts hints of lemon, mint, and smoke. There are two main types of cardamom: black cardamom and green cardamom. In baking, green cardamom pods are used.*

# JAMAICAN PUMPKIN PIE SPICE BLEND

## MAKES 8 TABLESPOONS

*In Jamaica, allspice is the baking spice of choice. On the island, it's known as pimento berries and flavors both baked goods and savory dishes, often alongside the herb thyme.*

| | | | |
|---|---|---|---|
| 4 | tablespoons ground cinnamon | ½ | teaspoon ground nutmeg |
| 2½ | tablespoons ground ginger | ¼ | teaspoon ground thyme |
| 4 | teaspoons ground allspice | ¼ | teaspoon ground black pepper |
| ½ | teaspoon ground mace | | |

1. In a small dry bowl, whisk ingredients together.
2. Place in an airtight container and store in a dry, cool, dark place.

# SPICY PUMPKIN PIE SPICE BLEND

**MAKES 8 TABLESPOONS**

*This sophisticated spice blend is reminiscent of spicy gingerbread in its flavor profile. It's gutsy, bold, and outrageously delicious. You'll love it!*

3 tablespoons ground ginger

2 tablespoons ground cinnamon

3 teaspoons ground allspice

1 teaspoon ground nutmeg

1 teaspoon dry mustard powder

1 teaspoon ground black pepper

1 teaspoon ground star anise

1 teaspoon ground anise

1 teaspoon ground cloves

1. In a small dry bowl, whisk ingredients together.
2. Place in an airtight container and store in a dry, cool, dark place.

# MEXICAN PUMPKIN PIE SPICE BLEND

**MAKES 8 TABLESPOONS**

*In Mexico, cinnamon, orange, chocolate, and other flavors often join together to create a sweet, spicy flavor profile.*

5 tablespoons ground cinnamon

1 tablespoon unsweetened cocoa powder

2 teaspoons ground allspice

2 teaspoons ancho chili powder

1 teaspoon ground ginger

1 teaspoon ground dried orange zest

1. In a small dry bowl, whisk ingredients together.
2. Place in an airtight container and store in a dry, cool, dark place.

# ABOUT THE AUTHOR

PHOTO BY ALYSSA PEEK OF PEEK PHOTOGRAPHY

**STEPHANIE PEDERSEN, MS, CHHC, AADP,** is a holistic nutritionist. A speaker and author of more than 20 books, Stephanie has a reputation for giving her clients the edge they need to get whatever they want from life. She does this by helping individuals to lose weight, manage food allergies, and detoxify naturally, using food and lifestyle changes.

As Stephanie says, "I want health for everyone! I have seen firsthand with myself and my own clients that when one works to get clean and fit and address your health challenges, life gets bigger. Suddenly, life becomes outrageously fun and easy. You move healthfully through life with ease."

According to Stephanie, getting healthy doesn't have to be complicated, or time-consuming. "As a mother, a writer, a nutritionist, a PTA mom, and someone who loves to have time alone to wander local farmer's markets, I know that complicated, overly-fussy diets, or an unnatural obsession with calorie-counting, are not the answers to getting and staying healthy." Instead, Stephanie espouses a life of love, laughter, daily exercise, and your favorite whole foods. "We're lucky that we live in a time when more and more gorgeous whole food ingredients, organic produce, and humanely farmed meat is available. Let's celebrate our good fortunate by exploring our many food and fitness options and experimenting with abandon!"

Pedersen currently lives in New York City with her husband and three sons. Visit her at **www.StephaniePedersen.com**

---

### ALSO BY STEPHANIE PEDERSEN:

*KISS Guide to Beauty: Keep It Simple Series*

· · · · · · · · · · · · · · · · · · · · · · · · · · · · · · · · · · · · · · · · · · · · · · · · · · · · ·

*Ginseng: Energy Enhancer*

· · · · · · · · · · · · · · · · · · · · · · · · · · · · · · · · · · · · · · · · · · · · · · · · · · · · ·

*Garlic: Safe and Effective Self-Care for Arthritis,*
*High Blood Pressure, and Flu*

· · · · · · · · · · · · · · · · · · · · · · · · · · · · · · · · · · · · · · · · · · · · · · · · · · · · ·

*Bra: A Thousand Years of Style, Support and Seduction*

# INDEX